MW01198810

17 well-known pieces for piano
by one of the world's greatest composers

TABLE OF CONTENTS

All selections on the CD are performed by
Valery Lloyd-Watts except where otherwise noted.

*Recorded by Chie Nagatani
**Recorded by Kim O'Reilly

Cover photo: © Horst Klemm / Masterfile

ISBN 0-7390-1723-3

Johann Sebastian Bach

Johann Sebastian Bach was born at Eisenach in Thuringia, Germany, on March 21, 1685. The same year saw the birth of the great Domenico Scarlatti as well as the renowned George Frideric Handel. J. S. Bach was a descendant of a long line of musicians. In Germany during that time, the name "Bach" had become almost synonymous with "musician."

Bach's parents died when he was only 10 years old. He was raised by his oldest brother, who was very jealous of Johann Sebastian's superior musical talents. He would not let the youngster use a musical book that he owned, which was filled with great compositions of master composers. The young Bach was able to get his hands on the book at night, however, by slipping it through the lattice-work doors of the book case in which it was locked. He copied it all by moonlight and damaged his eyesight permanently in doing so. When he discovered what the boy had done, the older brother took the copy away from him, but to no avail, since Johann Sebastian had already memorized the entire book!

At age 15, when his older brother died, Johann Sebastian became a choir boy at the school of St. Michael, in Luneberg, 200 miles away. In this new setting he was able to diligently study music and improve himself as a performer and composer.

At the age of 19 he accepted his first professional job as an organist, in a church at Arnstadt. Four years later he became organist at Mulhausen, where he married his cousin, Maria Barbara.

Bach's musical genius reached its greatest heights at Leipzig, Germany, where he was appointed cantor at the St. Thomas School, with responsibility for all the musical activities of its associated churches. In 1720 Maria Barbara died, and a year later Bach married Anna Magdalena Wilcken, a young singer who became a loving mother to Bach's family of 7 children, and bore him 13 more.

Bach's phenomenal output as a composer includes enough music to fill 46 volumes the size of an encyclopedia. He wrote hundreds of keyboard works, including music for clavichord, harpsichord and organ, as well as solos for violin, cello and other instruments. He also composed numerous instrumental duets, trios and orchestral works, and more than 250 sacred and secular cantatas. But the quality of his compositions is even more remarkable than the great quantity. No one has ever written greater music, particularly in the contrapuntal style, and Johann Sebastian Bach ranks as one of the towering musical geniuses of all time.

In 1725 Bach presented his wife, Anna Magdalena, with a beautiful notebook as a birthday present. In this book, Anna Magdalena, Johann Sebastian and other members of the family wrote many short and easy pieces that were either composed by Bach or were favorite pieces of the family. These are the simplest pieces we have from the family circle, and some of these are included on the following pages. In these pieces, there are often repeats of each half. It is customary to embellish (add trills, etc.,) on the repeats as heard on the recording.

After a long and prolific career, Bach died in Leipzig, Germany on July 28, 1750.

Aria

"Enlightening Thoughts of a Tobacco Smoker"

from the *Notebook for
Anna Magdalena Bach*

 Track 1

Menuet in G Major

Track 2

from the *Notebook for*
Anna Magdalena Bach

ⓐ Played:

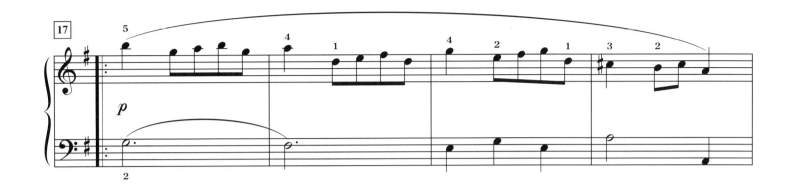

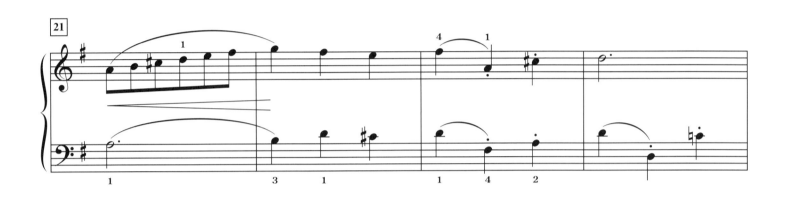

Menuet in G Minor

from the *Notebook for Anna Magdalena Bach*

Track 3

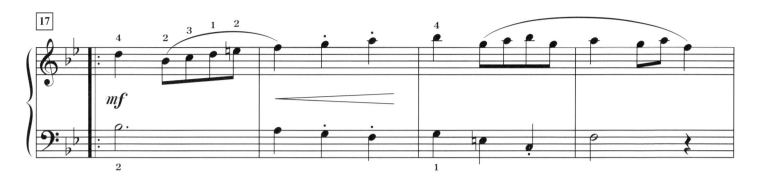

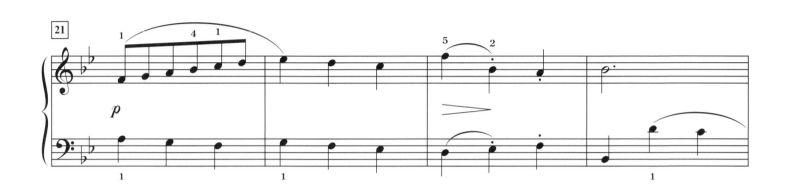

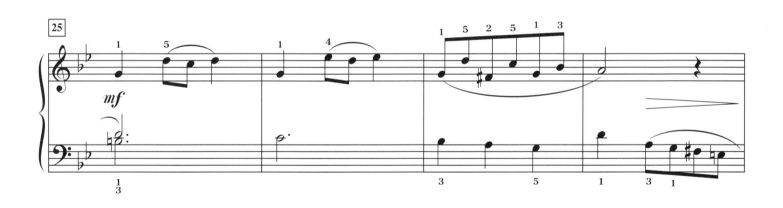

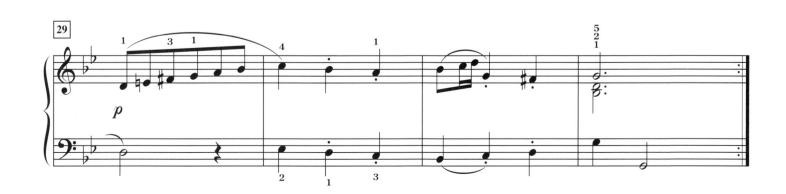

8

Musette in D Major

Track 4

from the *Notebook for*
Anna Magdalena Bach

March in D Major

Track 5

from the *Notebook for*
Anna Magdalena Bach

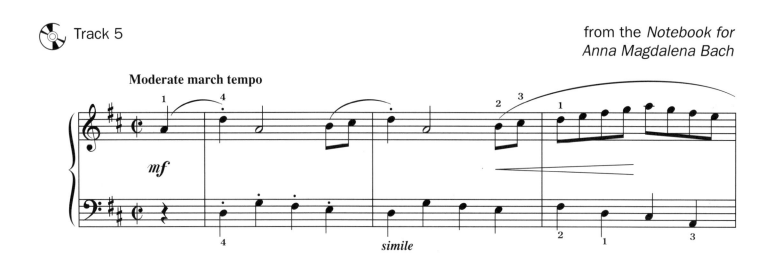

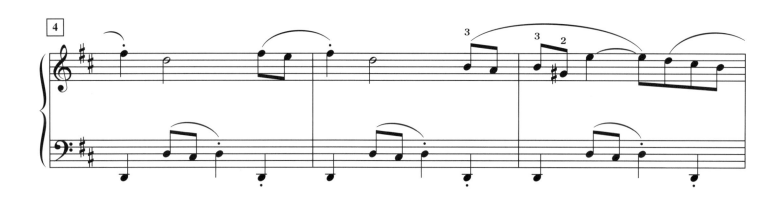

ⓐ Played:

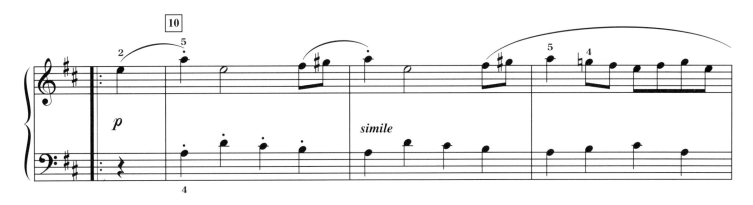

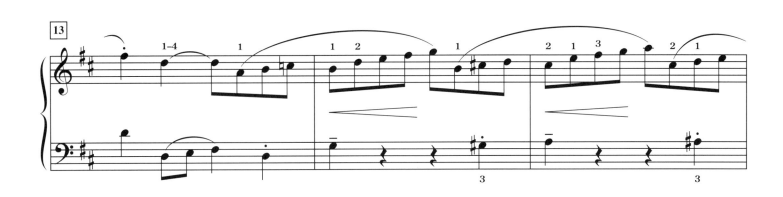

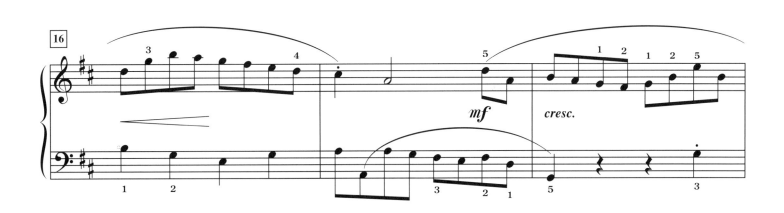

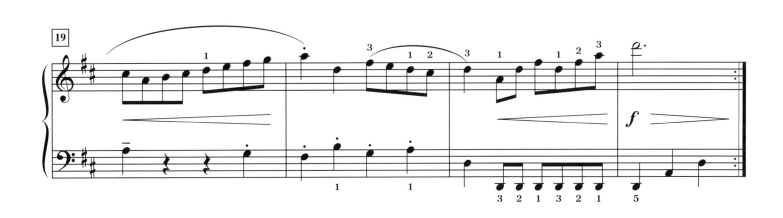

March in E♭ Major

from the *Notebook for Anna Magdalena Bach*

Track 6

ⓐ The trill may be played:

(b) The longer trill should be played:

Polonaise in G Minor

Track 7

from the *Notebook for Anna Magdalena Bach*

Allegro moderato

Chorale

"Be Content"

Track 8

from the *Notebook for Anna Magdalena Bach*

Musette

Track 9

from *English Suite No. 3 in G Minor*

Trio in G Minor

Track 10

from the *Little Clavier Book for W. F. Bach*

Andante moderato

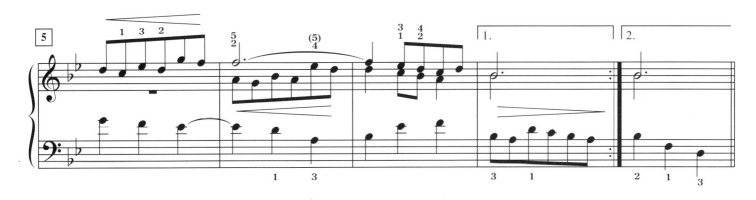

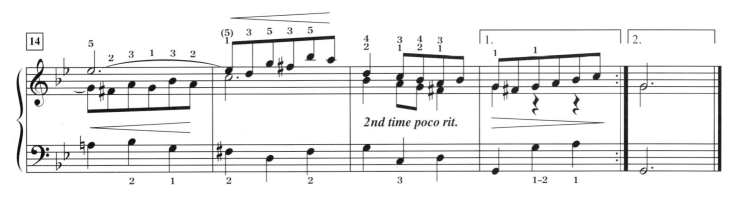

Aria

"When Thou Art Near"

Track 11

from the *Notebook for Anna Magdalena Bach*

Prelude in C Major

 Track 12

from the *Little Clavier Book for W. F. Bach*

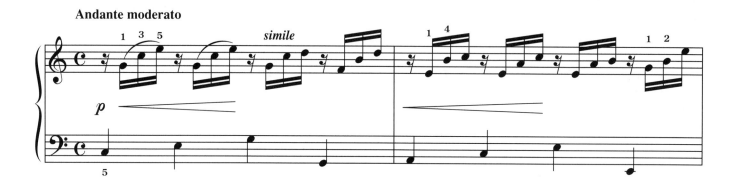

Prelude in C Major

Track 13

from 12 Short Preludes

Prelude in C Major

Track 14

from the *Well-Tempered Clavier*, Vol. I

Invention No. 1 in C Major

Track 15

from the
Two-Part Inventions

ⓐ Trills (⩘) should begin on the upper note: ⓑ Mordents (⩘) are played rapidly:

Bourrée

 Track 16

from the
Lute Suite in E Minor

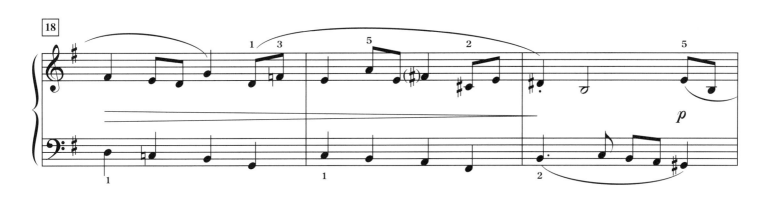

(a) Played:

Invention No. 8 in F Major

Track 17

from the
Two-Part Inventions

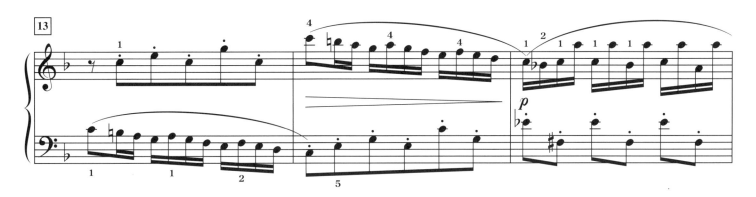

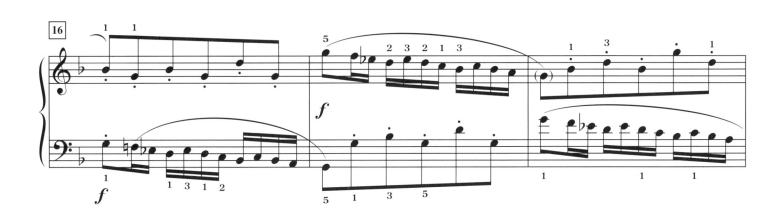

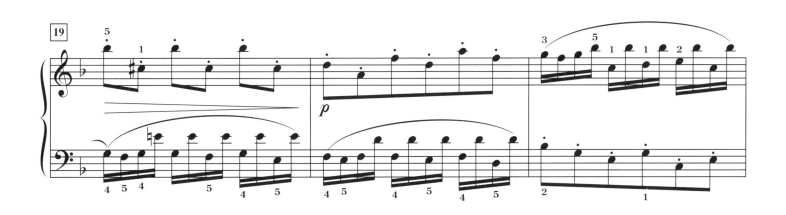

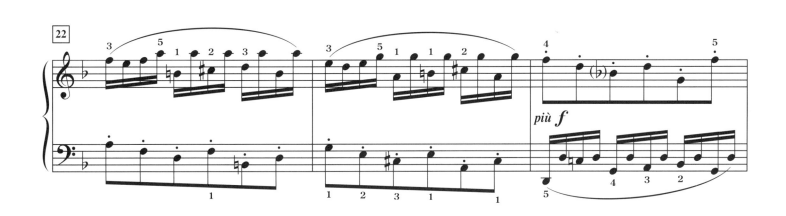

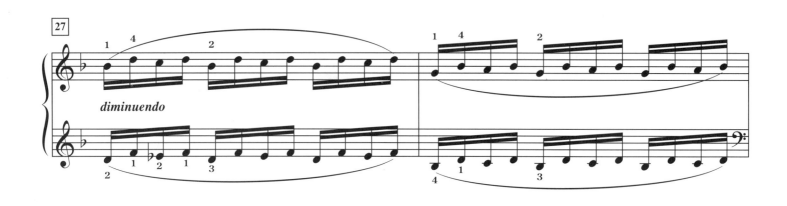

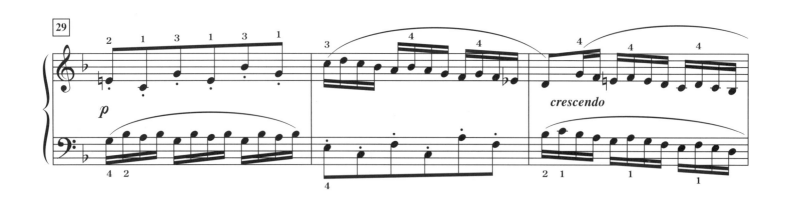